My Heart Leaps

a book of graphic psalms

Written and Illustrated by

Katherine Fortner Doerge

A NOTE ON SCRIPTURE REFERENCES:
Scripture references are not taken from any one translation. Some times a verse comes to mind in my own "paraphrased" version. Other times, I read several translations, and then express the passage in a personal form as God speaks it to my own heart. I refer to this as my "personalized" version.

MY HEART LEAPS
Arlington, TX
www.myheartleaps.com

ISBN-13: 978-0692316702

table of contents

For many years, I struggled in my spiritual life. I loved God and was committed to living a God-honoring life. I loved the Scriptures and I worked hard to develop some helpful spiritual disciplines: regular devotional time, Scripture reading and study, prayer and fasting, church involvement, and giving. Even with all my efforts, I was frustrated and confused in my relationship with God. Why did God seem so far away? Where was God anyway?

Only after going through a personal crisis did I discover the problem: I had lost touch with my own heart. Up until that time, I had thought that my heart was the problem. I thought it was something that needed to be suppressed...it certainly was a troublesome thing...all those emotions, desires, and dreams... often unmanageable and very unpredictable. And didn't Scripture say that the heart was "desperately wicked"? So I tried to keep it out of play as much as possible. However, after a time, this heart of mine, which I had neglected and tried to deny, would no longer be silenced. My heart cried out in anguish, and inexplicably a door opened and I was ushered into the very presence of God. For the first time in my life, I began to experience the intimacy with God I had longed for. As my heart opened, God began to touch and heal deep places in my soul. It was frightening and painful...but also life-changing and freeing. I was filled with a passion and life I had never known before.

Drawing, painting, and other forms of creative expression became outlets for me. They became ways of embracing, absorbing, and remembering the truths I was discovering... truths about myself, about life, and about God.

I don't know how I lost touch with my heart and missed this matter of the heart. The scriptures speak often of the heart and it's importance. We are told to love God, serve God, worship God, and love others, FROM THE HEART. In essence, we are to live all of life from the heart and it is with the heart that we commune with God. If we lose touch with our heart, we lose our very lifeline to God.

My Heart Leaps is a collection of drawings, paintings, scriptures, and words that have come to me as I have met with God in the private sanctuary of my own heart. As I honestly express my thoughts, my concerns, my struggles, my joys, my fears, my confusion...whatever is on my heart... a door opens to God's presence. My images and writing are chronicles of these encounters. They are fresh and raw...expressing real life, real pain, real struggles, and a real God who is intimately present in it all.

I am a "graphic psalmist". Psalmists intimately share their passion and life and how God meets them in the midst of it. When others read or sing what the psalmist writes, they get in touch with their own heart and come to know God's heart and presence in a deeper way. My desire is that when others see my graphic images they likewise will connect with their own heart and be drawn into an intimate encounter with God.

May joy fill your soul in God's embrace.

K. Doerge

I WILL NEVER LET YOU GO

K. Doerge

My heart cries out,

> "God, I'm doing everything I can!
> But it's not helping!
> I feel life slipping away but I can't stop it."

Such a difficult time... many changes, many losses.

> Each day I feel myself slipping into depression.
> I think, "I need to read my Bible more...I need to exercise...I need to eat better."

But all my efforts cannot spare me from the grieving I have to go through.

The few people with whom I have contact don't understand.

> "Trust the Lord." "Pray." "Rejoice in the Lord always...
> spend more time worshipping and praising."
> "You need to be serving."

Sundays are tough...I put on a good face and hope no one talks to me.

> I see her coming toward me but can't get away in time.
> "How are you doing? she asked.
> "I'm hanging in there."
> She admonishes me, "Don't just hang in there...
> you've got to stand, Girl! Stand on the Rock!"

With a tired look and a slight smile,

> I wobble both knees...no, I haven't much on which to stand.

"Oh God, I can't do this anymore!

> I'm struggling to just make it through the day.
> I'm trying to hold on but I'm falling. I'm falling!"

God whispers, *"I have hold of you dear child...rest in that truth. I will never let go of you."*

And in that moment, I realize that it does not depend on me holding on to God.

> The truth is that God is holding on to me and will never let me go.

> "Though I stumble, I will not fall,
> For the LORD holds me by the hand."
> Psalm 37:24

CALL OUT TO ME

Darkness and pain grips my whole being...no words.
    I pull my knees to my chest and wrap my arms around myself.
My heart beats in my throat...
A fury rushes in my head...
    storm winds rip and tear at my soul.

But then it quietens...my trembling body begins to relax.
    I lift my head and slowly open my eyes to see my friend,
        sitting with her hands clasped, head bowed in prayer,
            her face etched with pain.

God's presence envelopes me...healing begins to flow into my troubled soul.

A painful passage...
    yet God came to me in the midst of it...
        and my friend helped make the opening...
A rich lesson...
    It is God's Presence that brings healing and Presence is ushered in by prayer.

My heart inquires, "God, it seems like it should be a simple thing
    to come into Your presence.
    But so many things hinder...
        things in my heart and life that close my spirit.
            and the darkness itself comes in to oppress and thwart.
    I'm beginning to see....this is where prayer comes in.
    And perhaps, You set it up this way?"

God whispers, "*You have little to offer those who are hurting or struggling.*
    There's not much you can do, but you can pray. You can give comfort.
        You can share My heart and truth to bring hope.
Only one thing is needful: My Presence...
    it is Presence that brings peace, healing, hope, life...all that is needed.
My presence is ushered in by prayer...
    call out to Me and I will answer."

"Call out to Me and I will answer;
when you cry for help, I will say, 'I Am Here.'"
Isaiah 58:9

I Hold You Safely In My Hands

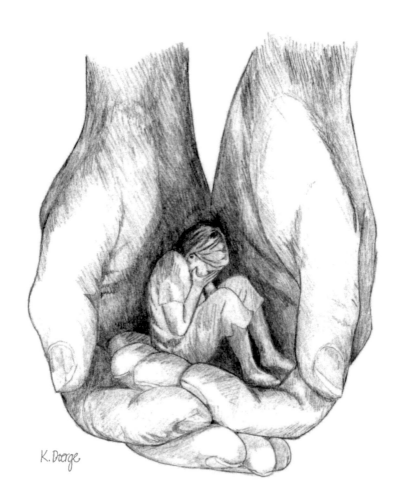

K. Doerge

My heart cries out,
  "Oh God, this is too painful.
    The grief is overwhelming.
  I am going to die...this will consume me.
        It is too much...it's unbearable."

God whispers,
  "You are my child in whom I delight. I will rescue you from all your enemies.
    I hold you safely in My Hands.
    I have seen you struggle and suffer and my heart is filled with compassion for you.
      I have spread My covering over you and have promised Myself to you...
          you are mine (Ezekiel 16:8).
    I have called you into My inner chamber...
        there you will find refuge in the secret place
            under the shadow of My wings (Psalm 91:1,4)."

      "God reached down and took hold of me,
        pulling me out of the trouble I was in,
    and delivering me from my enemies and all that tormented me.
          It was too much for me,
        But God was with me and helped me.
          I was delivered and
      brought out into a place of abundance...
        just because it delighted God to do it."
              Psalm 18:16-19

Yes, that's what I need, more than anything else...a safe place...a refuge in the midst of the storm.
  Storms will come...but God's presence is with me in the midst of my troubles...
        sheltering me and bringing me safely through.

"God, help me remember during those times that
        You are with me and holding me safely in Your hands."

    "Because you have set your love upon Me, I will deliver you;
  I will set you on high, because you have known My name. You shall call upon Me,
      and I will answer you; I will be with you in trouble;
        I will deliver you and honor you."
              Psalm 91:14,15

LET ME SEE YOUR FACE

It starts with a nagging foreboding feeling...something is wrong.
Then the changes...slight, then more pronounced.

Fear comes first...unexpected and surprising, "I've never been afraid to do this before."

Soon it creeps into daily activities, into dreams, into conversations,
I carefully guard myself to avoid the fear... the panic.
Then the tiredness... permeating my body as I struggle to rise in the morning,
as I yearn for a nap, as I watch the clock counting the minutes until bedtime.
"I just want to go to bed."

Finally, time for bed, but sleep doesn't come... endless, restless nights.
An awful dullness and boredom takes hold.

Food has no flavor, jokes and comedies are flat, romances at most elicit scorn.
I don't care anymore...I don't care about the things that used to be so very important to me.
Conversations with friends seem to be about nothing.

"Who cares about this? What difference does it make?"

Finally, I know...I can no longer ignore it...something is wrong, terribly wrong.
I feel alienated from my life, from my family, from my friends, from myself.
I'm angry at my body for betraying me, for rebelling against life as it has been.

My heart cries out, "Lord, what's happening to me? I don't understand!"

God whispers, *"Listen to your body...what is it saying?"*

It's screaming: "I can't do this anymore." "I'm sick and tired." "I need rest." "I hurt."

"Yes, something is wrong. Come to Me, dear child. Let me see your face...let me hear your voice...
I will reveal and restore."

"Oh my dove, hiding in the clefts of the rock, in the secret places of the cliff,
Let me see your face, Let me hear your voice;
I love hearing your sweet voice and seeing your lovely face."
Song of Songs 2:14

This "unveiling" is the beginning of God's healing work. No more pretense...I am NOT fine.
I am forced to face reality.. something is wrong and I cannot ignore it. It is a terrifying realization.

"With an unveiled face, I behold God's glory like a reflection in a mirror,
I am being transformed into the image of God, with greater and greater glory, by the Spirit."
2 Corinthians 3:18 (personalized)

"Oh, God, show me the way. Give me the strength and courage to open my heart and soul to healing.
Guide me to the people and resources I need."

YOU ARE MINE

"When I passed by you and looked at you,
I saw that it was your time for love;
So I spread My garment over you and covered your nakedness.
I made a promise to you and
entered into a covenant with you, and you became Mine."
Ezekiel 16:8

God, I lived hidden and alone for so long...
I wanted to draw close to You...but I held back...
I was like a little child hiding in the shadows, peering out...longing, desiring...
but afraid to reach out.

And it is so true...You did come to me and call me into love...
You so gently encompassed me and covered me in my vulnerability.

But even then, I held back. I stayed in the "outer" court...
safe and protected but not venturing into Your inner chamber.
I was afraid....Your light is so revealing.
I was afraid of what was within my own heart and soul.
I was also afraid of You.
I didn't know You then, like I know You now...I didn't know Your heart of love toward me.

Oh God, You have been so gracious and patient with me...I am so grateful.
You continued to draw me...You continued to woo me...
Until I opened to Your love and stepped through the curtain into Your intimate presence

Oh, yes, the Light penetrates and reveals, but in the revealing,
I come to know You....and me
in ways I've never known before.
Nothing compares to that inner knowing.

Thank you for calling me...calling me to be Yours.

God whispers, *"I have always known you and loved you. I created you to be Mine.*
It is my joy to bring you into my inner chamber. Indeed, your time is the time for love."

"The God who created you, And formed you, says this:
'Fear not, for I have redeemed you; I have called you by your name; You are Mine.'"
Isaiah 43:1

I Will Give You Water In The Desert

My heart cries, "God, I am so alone.
Everything has been stripped away...every comfort, everything familiar.
It's so desolate.
Why?"

God whispers, *"I have called you apart...to Myself.*
It may seem like a desolate place but I will care for you here.
I will heal you and restore you.
I will provide all that you need."

"Behold, I am doing a new thing...you will see it spring forth;
and know that it is by My hand.
I will make a way through the wilderness and provide water in the desert.
All creatures honor Me and know I provide for them.
I give water in the wilderness and make rivers in the desert,
To give drink to My people, My chosen ones.
This people I have formed for Myself to show forth My praise."
Isaiah 43:19-21

"God, I do know that You are with me...that You are in this place with me.
I know You will provide for me even when it seems so desolate.
Help me remember this when the hard times come...
when I'm hot and thirsty,
hungry and tired,
cold and exposed...
Help me remember that You will make a way...
that You will provide what I need in the wilderness.
And my part?
To trust you...to lean on You."

"Who is this coming up from the wilderness,
leaning upon her beloved?"
Song of Solomon 8:5

IT'S ME!!!

Leaning hard on my Beloved who is bringing me up from the wilderness.

WHY DO YOU SAY YOUR WAY
IS HIDDEN FROM ME?

My heart cries,
        "God, don't you know what I'm going through? Where are You?"

God whispers,
        "I am here. I have always been with you.
                I have seen your wanderings. I have seen your tears.
        But more than that, I always carry you close to My heart.
                I know your struggle...I know your sorrow...I know your fear...
                        I am with you and I will see you through it all."

                "Why do you say:
        'My way is hidden from God, and my just claim is ignored by my God?'
                Don't you know? Haven't you heard?
                I am the eternal God, The Creator of the earth.
                I am attentive and always at work,
                seeing and knowing more than you can fathom."
                        Isaiah 40:27-28

And suddenly, I realize: I am asking the wrong questions.
                Obviously, God does see, God does know.
        So my questions really should be:
                "God, where are You in this?
                        What is Your purpose in this place?"

"God, I believe You do see...
                You know what is going on in my life.
        And You have heard my cries...You are with me...You aren't ignoring me.
                Help me to see You in this."

                "You see my all wanderings, every struggle.
        You keep an account of all I go through, you even collect up the tears I shed.
                When I cry out to You, my enemies turn away;
                        One thing I know: You are for me...
                        I trust You and am not afraid.
                        What can anyone do to me?
                        I will be faithful to You and praise You,
        For You have sustained me and preserved My life."
                        Psalm 56:8-13

I Am God and I Am With You

"I'm in trouble and calling out to You, O God;
In Your mercy, hear my prayer."
Psalm 130:1,2

My heart cries,
"God, I'm not handling this very well. Why does it affect me so?
Am I really so untrusting? Am I really so fearful? Am I really so fragile?"

I feel like my body is betraying me.
My mind says, "Trust God." But my body is in pain.
My heart is in anguish.
My soul gropes and staggers about like a seaman wrestling the sails
in the midst of a storm. I strain to stay on course.

God whispers,
"Come here, Dear One. Come here. Why so much confusion?
Your body is not betraying you.
The truth is that your body is refusing to let YOU betray it.
For you see, trust is not about denying reality...
trust is about accepting reality.
The reality is that you are in the midst of a storm.
The reality is that you are fragile and vulnerable...
You are human.
Trust begins with accepting this reality.
The other reality is that I am God and I am with you."

"Yes, you are hard pressed, but I won't let you be crushed.
Yes, you are perplexed, but I will not let you be consumed by despair.
Yes, you are aggrieved, but I will not let you be forsaken.
You may be struck down, but I will not let you be destroyed.
(2 Corinthians 4:8-10 personalized)
Call out to me when you're in trouble...
I will hear you and be with you.
In the midst of the pressure, the confusion, the grief, and the pain, I am God."

"Because we have this treasure in fragile human vessels,
there's no mistaking that it's from God, and not from ourselves."
2 Corinthians 4:7

I KNOW WHAT YOU'RE GOING THROUGH

Such a difficult time...moving so far away...away from family and friends...
tremendous losses...
so many changes in my life.
The grief and isolation are overwhelming.

Feeling intensely alone and desperate,
I decide to get out of the house to clear my head.
I put on my jogging clothes and head out for a run.

As I run, I pour out my heart out to God....how alone I feel...
and how overwhelmed I am with all the changes.

I look up at the clouds as I run. As I watch the clouds change and move,
a scripture passage comes to mind:
the vision that Steven saw when he was being stoned.

"Look! I see heaven open and
the Son of Man standing at the right hand of God!"
Acts 7:56

God whispered, *I know what you are going through.*
I am very aware of your pain and struggle and I am with you.

Jesus standing at God's right hand...standing...not sitting.
In Stephen's time of great need and suffering, Jesus is standing.
Jesus has risen to His feet in response to the suffering of his beloved child.

At that moment, I know that God is very aware of my struggle
and there with me.

God does indeed know what we are going through...
God is intimately present.

Calling out to God and honestly acknowledging my humanness and vulnerability
creates an opening for God's presence to flow into my life.
and that makes all the difference.

Bring Me Your Passion

"God, there is such awfulness inside.
It is so strong and intense. I suppose it must be called rage.
I don't like it...but I can't shake it...it is as though sinews attach it to my very soul.
Help me."

I pour out my distress...my fury and despair.
Beneath my anger and rage are grief and loss.
But there's nothing I can do to shake it.
There's no way to go back...no way to undo what's been done.

My heart cries, "God, I need your healing. You are my only hope."

God whispers, *"Open your heart to Me.*
Bring me your passion...your joys, your pain, even your rage...
it is the doorway into My Presence.
Allow Me to touch the inner places so in need of healing. "

"But God, how can you stand me like this?
I can't stand it myself. Why would You want me to come around at all.
But what else can I do? I can't make it go away...nor can I deny it."

God whispers,
"I can handle your anger and rage...even when you lash out at Me.
I see the pain and loss beneath it all...
allow me into Your heart that I might bring healing. Will you allow Me in?"

"I was so foolish and horrible; I was like a wild animal.
But still You are with me, holding on to me.
You help me find a way though those tough times and restore me.
You are the only One for me, in heaven or on earth.
I will have struggles and failures in this life,
But You are the strength of my life and my greatest gift."
Psalm 73:22-26

"Cry out to Me when you're in trouble.
Pour out your complaints and woes to Me.
When you're feeling overwhelmed and defeated,
I am with you to guide you. "
Psalm 142:1

Your Home Is With Me

"God, I feel like I don't have a home.
I don't feel like I belong anywhere."

God whispers,
"Your home is with Me. This is your true home.
Remember I have called your heart My home.
I am always at home with you in the inner sanctuary of your heart."

"The sparrow has found a home,
And the swallow a nest for herself,
Where she may raise her young—
near Your sanctuary, Oh God,
Blessed are those who live in Your Presence;
They will continually praise You."
Psalm 84:3,4

One of my favorite characters is Horton the Elephant from the Dr. Seuss book,
Horton Hears A Who.
He's kind of my own personal mascot because of our shared mission...
to convince others that another world exists...
a world that is real and worthy of our focus.

Horton's other world was this tiny, almost invisible civilization of Who's...
mine is the immense, unseen spiritual world.
At times, I feel like ole Horton...
telling others about this "other world"
and wondering if I am perceived as ridiculous and crazy as Horton was.

Just like Horton, I cannot forsake this other world...
I am on a mission:
"HEY! There's another world...the spiritual world...unseen and mysterious..
but oh so real and full of life...vibrant, abundant life.
Feel it...taste it...see it...experience it!"

Not only does this other world exist...it is our true home.

I WILL MAKE A WAY

"You know, God, I didn't like the desert at first...it seemed so barren and harsh.
And too open...I felt exposed.
But it seems different now. I've come to like this place.
Yes, it is lonely sometimes...but the peace and solitude are nice.
And there's a beauty and a freedom I have never known before."

I am learning so much about living in the desert...that lonely desolate place.
I'm learning to accept it and see that there is more here than I had expected.
I am learning more and more about the beauty and bounty here...
a rich aliveness that cannot be possessed...
often hidden and transient...and rarely duplicated.

I'm a bit resistant to the concept of viewing this life as a journey through a desert.
And yet...we don't belong here...
we are strangers in this world
so it makes sense that we would experience life here
as being somewhat hostile and desolate like the desert.
Oh, yes, we have those times when we come upon an oasis...
cool and welcoming, restful and refreshing...but we cannot stay long.
We must continue on our journey, on to the next place and the next lesson prepared for us.

"God, I love that you journey with Me...
providing what I need...nourishing me...protecting me...guiding me...teaching me.
And then there are those special times when You bring others along the way
who touch me with Your love and comfort that reach to the depth of my soul.
And I am strengthened and given courage to continue on...
to the next place...the next lesson."

"Behold, I am doing a new thing...you will see it spring forth;
and know that it is by My hand.
I will make a way through the wilderness and provide water in the desert.
All creatures honor Me and know I provide for them.
I give water in the wilderness and make rivers in the desert,
To give drink to My people, My chosen ones.
This people I have formed for Myself to show forth My praise."
Isaiah 43:19-21

MAKE ME A SANCTUARY

"Make Me a sanctuary that I may dwell with you."
Exodus 25:8

"Oh God, You're incredible! First, You choose a people for Yourself.
You become their own personal God.
You lead them out of bondage and bring them to a new land...
And THEN You tell them that You want to dwell with them...to be with them always!
How amazing!"

And with that I realize another truth:
In the same way, God comes to each of us and says,
"Make Me a sanctuary that I may dwell with you."

God desires to dwell with us!!! How wonderful!
We are to prepare a sacred place for the Divine within our own hearts.
A holy dwelling place within...like the Garden of Eden where we
walk with God "in the cool of the day"...an intimate place of communion.

Scripture speaks of a time when Israel will be like a well-watered garden...
so we also are to become like a well-watered garden.

"God, I understand now about this intimate place within that is reserved for You alone.
I know it is a sacred place but
I'm not really sure how to nurture and preserve this sanctuary within...
this place of communion with You."

God whispers, *"Indeed, I have called you to make a sanctuary for Me that
I might dwell with You. That is My heart's desire.
I will show you how to tend this garden and how to protect it.
I will cause it to flourish and grow.
I will delight to walk with you there in the cool of the day."*

*"I will guide you continually,
And satisfy your soul in drought,
I will renew and strengthen you;
You will be like a well-watered garden,
And like a spring of water that never fails."*
Isaiah 58:11

REMAIN IN THE LIGHT OF MY PRESENCE

"God, you have done so much in me...I see it in the familiar things that now seem so different."

"Like waking up the other night from that dream I've had so many times...
　　　　　but this time it was different...
　　There was no panic..
　　　　　　　　Instead there is a quietness...
　　　　　　　　a stillness...
　　　　　　　　　　　a light...Your Light
　　　　　　　　　　　　　shining over me.
　　I am safe and secure. There is a way through this.
　　　　　　Your Light is there... protecting... guiding... permeating the darkness.
　　Yes, there are dangers in the darkness
　　　　　　　　　　but in the Light they are no threat.
　　　　　　　　　　　　They cannot overcome the Light."

God whispers, *"Remain in the Light of My presence...I will show you the way."*

"I will lead you by a way you have not known; I will guide you along a new path.
I will make darkness light before you, And will smooth out the rough places.
You can trust Me to do this for you."
Isaiah 42:16

"Whether you turn to the right or the left,
You will hear a voice behind you saying,
'This is the way, walk in it.'"
Isaiah 30:21

"God, I am so amazed and thankful!
　　　　Thankful that You are with me, showing the way.
　　Even when the path is unknown and dark,
　　　　You are there, shining Your light into the darkness, guiding me."

God whispers,
"Because you have set your love upon Me, therefore I will deliver you;
I will set you on high, because you have known My name.
You shall call upon Me, and I will answer you; I will be with you in trouble;
I will deliver you and honor you. With long life I will satisfy you, and show you My salvation."
Psalm 91:14-16

I WILL MEET YOU IN THIS PLACE

" As the deer longs for water,
So my soul longs for You, O God.
My soul thirsts for You, the living God..."
Psalm 42:1,2

Lovely imagery...
    the deer panting for the waters...intimate longing for communion with God.
I sweetly sing the chorus:
    "As the deer panteth for the water,
        so my soul longeth after Thee..."

But what does it mean to experience this?
    Have I allowed myself to know the depth of this longing within?

My heart cries, "God, this deep longing within...
    this thirst...it is uncomfortable... even frightening in a way.
        It feels very lonely. But there is something that draws me to this place."

God whispers,
    "Yes, you must know the depths of this longing...this aloneness...
        it is this intimate place within that I desire to touch.
            At first it seems an empty, painful place...
        but as you accept it,
    you will find it to be a place of peace and quietness that brings rest to your soul.
I will meet you in this place and
        you will come to know Me and life in a way you could not know otherwise."

Taste the thirst within...allow yourself to experience this deep longing.
    Painful, yes...but rich and beautiful...
        and the opening for God's intimate presence and provision.

"O God, You are my God; I will pursue You;
My soul thirsts for You; My body longs for You
In a dry and barren land where there is no water."
Psalm 63:1

MY PRESENCE WILL GO WITH YOU

"Moses said, 'God, if Your Presence doesn't go with us, don't move us from here.'"
"So God said to Moses, 'I will do what you have asked;
for you have found favor in My sight, and I know you by name.'"
Exodus 33:15,17

"I love that, God....that You would promise to be with Your people,
to go with them and bring them to a place of rest.
I also love Moses' heart…
that he doesn't want to go anywhere unless Your presence is with them."

"That's what I want too. I only want to be where you are God.
But how does it happen? How do we remain in Your presence?"

Surely, prayer is how that happens...
...but there seems to be some confusion about prayer...
I'm pretty sure it's NOT about claiming something we think God owes us...
nor is it some exercise in building our faith to believe for what we want.
I see it more as making an opening for God to come into our life...
inviting God's presence in to fill "the temple".
And, oh, what a difference that makes! It is God's presence that heals.
God's presence brings peace...
God's presence brings hope...joy...rest...and so much more.
In a way, who cares what happens to us, if God is with us?

What matters most is God being PRESENT WITH US!!!
So, to me, that's the call...making that opening for God's presence...drawing close...
remaining in God's presence...
and not moving from any place lest Holy Presence goes with me.
That's a lesson from Moses and the children of God in the wilderness...
the pillar of fire at night...the cloud by day...God's presence with them...
leading them...protecting them.

My heart cries, "Oh God, that's what I want: Your presence with me, leading and guiding me.
Only in Your presence does my soul find what it needs...
peace...joy...love...healing...hope...and sweet rest."

God whispers, *"I will show you the path of life; In My presence is fullness of joy;*
At My right hand are pleasures forevermore." Psalm 16:11

I AM YOUR ROCK

"God is my rock, my fortress and my deliverer."
2 Samuel 22:2

"From the furthest reaches of the earth, I will cry out to You,
when I am overwhelmed and weary, lead me to the rock that is higher than I."
Psalm 61:2

"God, what does it mean for You to be My Rock?"

God whispers, *"I am your Rock. I am the only immovable, unchanging reality in this life.*
I am the One sure thing in all of life.

I am your Rock…your savior rescuing your soul from danger.
(Psalm 62:1)
I am your Rock…your stronghold anchoring you when the storms rage.
(Psalm 62:7)
I am your Rock…your protection lifting you above your enemies around you.
(Psalm 27:5,6)
I am your Rock…your hiding place sheltering you in
the cleft I have made for you. (Song of Solomon 2:14)
I am your Rock…your stumbling stone crushing fear and doubt. (1 Peter 2:8)
I am your Rock…your Maker giving you life and breath. (Deuteronomy 32:18)
I am your Rock…your provision quenching the thirst of your soul.
(1 Corinthians 10:4,5)
I am your Rock…your companion guiding you along
your journey toward home. (1 Corinthians 10:4)

It is comforting and frightening at the same time. Oh, yes, the Rock gives me life, protects me, hides me, saves me, guides me. The Rock is faithful, dependable, immovable. But as surely as the Rock shields and protects, it can crush and expose. For this Rock is the great I AM…sovereign, mighty God.

Come to the Rock…find shelter and protection…find life…but never, ever resist the Rock.

"Be mindful of the Rock who begot you,
Don't forget the God who created you."
Deuteronomy 32:18

I WILL PLANT YOU IN THIS LAND

"God, you have brought me through so much.
But now I'm in a place that seems so unfamiliar.
I feel like I'm a different person with new responses to things.
I'm more in touch with my heart and so aware of Your presence with me...in me.
It's like I'm a new person, in a new place.
How do I live here?"

"Build houses, plant gardens..."

I remembered these words from scripture and knew the context:
Israel has been taken into exile and God says something like:
"You're going to be here for a while...
settle down and make it home..."

I open the scriptures to read more and hopefully understand God's heart in these words.
I don't find the passage that came to mind...
Instead, I come to one that is similar but very different.

"I will bring you back from captivity;
You will rebuild the cities and live there;
You will plant vineyards and drink wine from them;
You will plant gardens and eat the produce from them.
I will plant you in your own land,
And no longer shall you be pulled up
from the land I have given you."
Amos 9:14,15

God whispers, *"Yes, this is what I have for you this time.*
I have brought you here and
you shall not be pulled up from the land I have given you."

What a gift...
to have the assurance that
what God has done in my life is permanent and eternal...
I can't lose it nor can it be taken away from me.

I HAVE CARRIED YOU

K. Doerge

"Oh, God, looking back on my journey, I can see now what I could not see along the way.
I can see Your Presence in my life...even in the things that seemed disastrous at the time.
But I didn't know You were there.
I made choices and decisions to protect myself, to survive."

It's so painful to come to terms with how much damage I did to myself and others
because of the choices and decisions I made in reaction to those times.

In anguish, my heart cries out, "God, this is too much to bear.
It's overwhelming...I feel so guilty and have so much regret!"

God whispers, *"Yes, it is too much to bear. That's why I sent Jesus...to bear your burden."*

Then I see it: God's incredible GRACE.
GOD KNEW ALL ALONG! God knew what my choices and decisions would be
and how they would impact me and others.

My heart leaps,
"God, You knew all along!
You knew what baggage I would take on.
You knew how it would affect me and my relationships with others...
and You used it to bring about Your Divine will in my life as well as theirs!
You knew all along and wove it all into the fabric of my life and the lives of those my life touches.
How amazing!"

"All things work together for the good of those who love God,
according to God's plan and purpose." Romans 8:28

"God has carried you, as a father carries his child,
all the way you went until you reached this place." Deuteronomy 1:31

God whispers, *"I have always loved you. I called you out of darkness and to Myself long ago.
I tenderly held your arms and taught you to walk. You didn't know it was Me.
I have led you... cared for you... healed you... provided for you.
I have taken your burdens from you. My compassion for you overflows."*
Hosea 11:1-8

Let Me Gather You

"The one who lives in the secret place of the Most High
is shielded and protected by God's Mighty power.
I say to God, 'You are my refuge and my fortress;
My God, in You will I trust.'"
Psalm 91:1,2

"God, I want to live in that secret place.
I guess that's just it...it is secret...no one but You and me.
It's funny how I want someone else, something else, in there...
but when I look for something else,
I am drawn away from what I really long for.
At first, it seems lonely and desolate,
but as I wait, I become aware of Your tender presence.
Your peace envelopes me...oh, how my soul is satisfied."

God whispers,
*"Yes, dear one, it is a delight for Me to gather you to Myself...
to settle you into the place of peace and rest
under My protective care.
Trust in My sufficiency and strength."*

"God, I don't really know why coming to You isn't my first response.
It seems that I have to struggle and exhaust myself before
I allow you to gather me in...
even then, I sometimes resist.
Oh, that I would remember this amazing place you have for me."

*"How often I wanted to gather you to Myself,
like a mother hen gathers her chicks under her wings..."*
Matthew 23:37

*"I will cover you with My feathers and
under My wings you shall find refuge.
My faithfulness will be your shield and protection."*
Psalm 91:4

BRING IT ALL TO ME

I was thinking about what happens when we go through intense times...
whether good or bad...
we clench our hands.
We do this when we are hurt, or scared, or angry...
but also if we are really excited...
we squeal with delight and clench our hands.
But with clenched hands we cannot receive.

That's when we must come to God and make the great exchange.
The great exchange is when I open my hands to God
offering up my anger, my fear, my sin, my resentment...
whatever is on my heart.
I offer it all up to God and in exchange,
God pours out Divine love, peace, hope, joy...
whatever my heart needs. Wow! What a deal!

"You know, God, with this exchange, you're getting a raw deal!"

God whispers, *"Yes, dear child...I know very well how raw it is...*
that is what Jesus suffered and endured on the Cross.
But in the exchange, I also get you...and that means the world to Me."

So the key is unclenching my hands...
and that comes as I honestly acknowledge my pain,
my fear, my confusion,
my disappointment, my failure...
anything that grips me.

But then with open hands, I am able to receive all God has for me.

And though my troubles do not go away,
they are transformed by God's life-giving presence
as I unclench my hands and offer them up.

"My eyes are worn out from crying because of my affliction.
God, I call out to You daily;
I stretch out my hands to You."
Psalm 88:9

REST IN THE PALM OF MY HAND

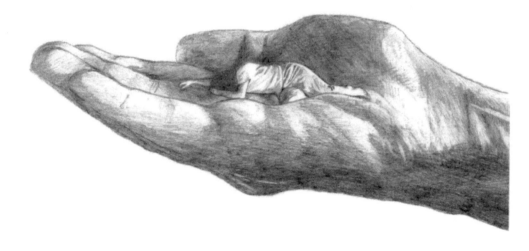

K. Doerge

"I remember You when I'm lying in bed,
I meditate on You during the night.
Because You help me, I rejoice in the shelter of Your protective wings,
I cling to you with my whole being; You hold me securely in Your right hand."
Psalm 63:6-8

"God, I'm so glad I can call out to You and know You are there.
Even in the night when things seem so dark and confusing, You are there.
But I don't always remember that.
I remember other things...
things I'm worried about, my fears, my disappointments, my frustrations.
God, I need to remember that You are there,
that You are upholding me, that You are sustaining me."

God whispers, *"Yes, dear child, rest in the palm of My hand.*
See, I have made a place for you here.
It is a place of rest...a place of safety...
a place of peace...a place of remembrance."

"God, it's so easy to forget.
When those dark times come, help me remember You...
to think of You through the watches of the night...
and find my resting place in the palm of Your hand."

God whispers, *"Though you may forget, I will never forget you...*
I have you engraved on the palms of My Hands. You are continually before Me."

"Can a woman forget her nursing baby,
And not have compassion on her own child?
Even though she may forget, I will never forget you.
See, I have you imprinted on the palms of My hands,
your form is ever before Me."
Isaiah 49:15,16

"Do not be afraid, for I am with you; Don't be disturbed or distressed, for I am your God.
I will strengthen you and help you,
I will hold you up with My righteous right hand."
Isaiah 41:10

LET YOUR LIGHT SHINE

My heart cries, "God, I so need your light.
I need Your light to dispel the darkness...
I need You to show me the way."

"You are the light of the world."

"God I don't get it. How am I 'the light of the world'?"

"You are the light of the world. A city on a hill cannot be hidden.
Nor does someone light a lamp and then cover it,
No, they put it up so that it gives light to all who are in the house."
Matthew 5: 14, 15

"And how does the light within me give 'light to all who are in the house'?
I don't get it.
God, I don't have anything to offer...this is so much bigger than I am.
I don't have a clue about how this is to work."

God whispers, *"I have placed My Light in you. Your only job is to let it shine.*
You must allow My Light to shine forth from within.
Your part is to not hinder My Light from shining...
'Put it under a bushel, NO!'
This is the way I have chosen to bring My Light and Love into the world.
I will show you...listen to My Spirit."

And so God gently guides me...

"Speak honestly from a loving heart." Ephesians 4:15

"Divine wisdom is first pure, then peaceable and gentle,
willing to yield and full of compassion,
impartial and sincere."
James 3:17

"Oh, God, I do want Your Light to shine forth.
My world needs it! I need it!
We need Your peace and grace, Your mercy and love.
Reveal the things that hinder Your Light from shining forth from me."

I HAVE SET YOU FREE

My heart leaps,
"Oh, God, how I want to fly...to experience true freedom and life.
So many things have weighed me down...
but You have lifted so much of that off of me as You have touched me
and brought truth and healing to my soul.
I do feel like I could fly
but I really don't know how to live this life of freedom.
It's all so very new."

God whispers, *"Yes, dear one, it is your time to fly.*
Remember it is my Spirit that is the wind that will lift and carry you.
You do not fly by your own strength...
your part is to make the delicate wing adjustments...
gentle...slight movements in response to My leading.
The key is staying intimately aware of My presence...
I will teach you the gentle art of riding the wind...My Spirit.
It is my delight to see you soar on wings like eagles."

How I've wanted to experience true freedom!
But my soul was laden with worries and fears,
wounds and disappointments, anger and resentments.
As I am opening my soul to God's healing touch,
these burdens are being lifted and I am being set free.
I'm realizing though that this is only the beginning.
Then come the flight lessons...learning to stay in God's intimate presence...
opening myself to the gentle wind of the Spirit to lift and carry me...
and soaring by God's strength and grace.

"I set you free so you could live in freedom.
Hold on to your freedom and don't go back into bondage."
Galatians 5:1

"As you trust in Me, your strength will grow;
You will rise up with wings like eagles..."
Isaiah 40:31

I'm still a bit cumbersome and have had my share of crash landings,
but I'm hooked on flying and am always ready for the next set of lessons!

LISTEN TO YOUR HEART

K. Doerge

My heart cries,
"God, just show me the way through this.
I know what the scriptures say but I still don't know what I should do.
Show me, God, show me."

"Send out Your light and Your truth, let them guide me;
let them bring me to Your Presence, to the place where you dwell."
Psalm 43:3

It would be nice if things were all mapped out...nicely laid out for me.
Most of the time, I'm not sure which way I should go or what I should do.
I ask for direction and guidance.
I read scripture...I listen for an answer...I look for a "sign".
Sometimes I get clarity, but often I don't.

"So what's the deal, God? Do I just take a shot?
Do I step out and hope I'm doing the right thing?
Isn't there some way to know or at least have an idea about which way to go?"

God whispers,
*"Listen to your heart. I have set your heart as a compass to guide and direct you.
Trust My Spirit within to lead you along the unique path I have chosen for you."*

*"I will give you a new heart and put a new spirit in you;
I will take your stony heart and give you a heart that is healthy and fully alive.
I will put My Spirit within you and you will know my heart and walk in My ways."*
Ezekiel 36:26,27

And so I find a quiet place away from the noise, inside and out.
Here I search my heart...I wait and listen. What do I know deep within?
What do I know in my gut?
I begin to realize that I know much more than I realized.

I guess it's really a matter of trust.
I must trust that God has indeed given me a new heart and a new spirit
that help guide me and direct me along my unique path.

*"I will give you counsel;
Your heart also will instruct you in dark times."*
Psalm 16:7

MY PROMISES ARE FOR
YOU AND YOUR CHILDREN

My heart speaks,
  "God, it's not easy going through tough times, but I'm learning.
      I know You will see me through. Even in the most difficult and painful times,
          You are there. I know that…I've experienced that.
  But, God, with the kids it's so hard. I don't want them to suffer.
      They don't have the resources I have…they can't see beyond the loss and pain.
      I'm it for them. I'm the one who has to be there for them.
          God, I'm struggling and hurting, how can I care for them?
              How can I protect them?"

God whispers, *"My promises are for you and your children.*
              I will be there for them just as I have been there for you.
                  I will give you what you need for them.
      And when you have no more to give,
          remember that My provision will be there for them just as it is for you.
              All that is dear to you, is dear to Me.
      My promises are for you AND your children."

Over and over, I see it in scripture:

"All the land that you see I will give to you and your children forever." Genesis 13:15
"I am establishing an everlasting covenant with you,
      between Me and you and your children for all generations to come…" Genesis 17:7
"May God give increase to both you and your children." Psalm 115:14
"The promise is for you and your children…" Acts 2:39

God, thank you for Your promises.
      Thank you for the assurance that You will provide not only for me but also for my children.
          That you will be there for them just as you have been there for me.
Help me teach them to look for You and see you in the midst of our lives.
      Help me share the story of Your faithfulness…
          so that they will hear the testimony of Your love for us…so that I don't forget.

          "Keep these words which I command you today in your heart.
              Teach them diligently to your children,
      Talk about them when you sit around home, when you're out and about,
              when you go to bed and when you get up."
                  Deuteronomy 6:6,7

DON'T BE AFRAID TO LOVE

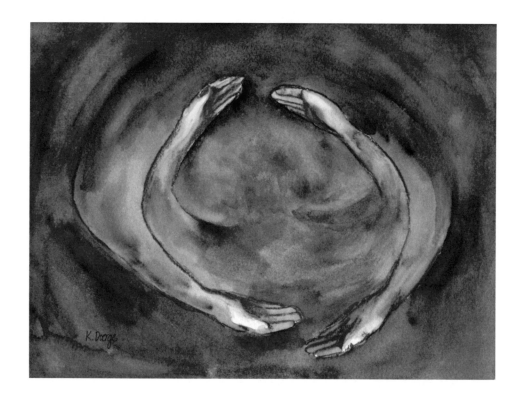

"God, what is it that causes relationships to be so complicated and confusing?
We seem to get so caught up with ourselves and what we want and need
that we miss out on what You have for us.
And then there's disappointment and anger.
How do you love with all that going on?"

God whispers, *"Don't be afraid to love.*
For it is in loving that you truly are who I created you to be.
But don't get confused about love.
True love is My light radiating from within you…
it is not something you do or give.
It is My radiance expressed through the unique person I created you to be."

Love seems very much like worship.
Just as I am to worship in spirit and truth,
I am to love in spirit and truth.
It flows from the center of my being…from my spirit.
Loving in truth requires an honest acceptance of who I am.
As I acknowledge my uniqueness and vulnerability,
my spirit opens to love…
to God's embrace and delight.
And as I find myself in God in this way,
I am able to see and express God's embrace and delight for others…
which is what true love is about.

When I say, "I love you," to another, in essence I am saying,
"I see you and I delight in the unique person God has created you to be."

It is really very simple.

But first, I must experience this delight for myself.
Then I testify with the psalmist:

"Thank you, God, for making me the way you did…unique and perfectly me;
I see the wonder and wisdom of your work!"
Psalm 139:14

MAY I HAVE THIS DANCE?

God whispers, *"Dance with Me."*

My heart questions, "Me? You want to dance with me? I don't get it."

"You are my beloved child.
    I knew you before you were born...I created you.
        You are a delight to Me. I rejoice over you with singing.
      My love brings peace to your soul.
    For it is in Me that you live and breathe and have your being.
      You are My child, My offspring.
    I love being with you.
      I love hearing your voice...so sweet!
        I love seeing your face...so beautiful!"
      (Zephaniah 3:17; Acts 17:28; Song of Solomon 2:14)

My heart leaps, "God, it's overwhelming to realize that You delight in me...
    that it brings You joy to be with me....
    that You take pleasure in my smile, my laughter, the sparkle in my eyes...
    that You would want to take my hand and dance with me.

    What a delight!
      For both of us...how amazing!"

"There's just one thing: I never learned to dance."

"All the better...just follow My lead."

"I have always loved you;
With tender love I have drawn you and pursued you.
I will build you up again and restore you...
You shall again be adorned with your tambourines,
And shall go forth in the dances of those who rejoice."
Jeremiah 31:3,4

YOU ARE A PRAYER

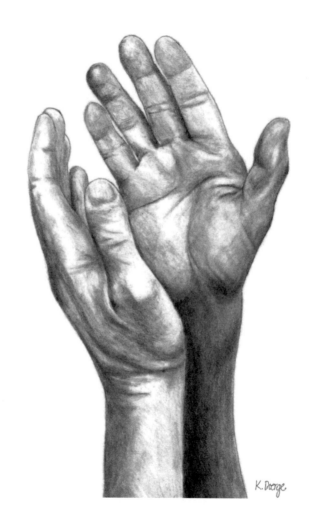

"God, I'm not really sure how prayer works.
I certainly know it's not about me talking You into something.
I'm actually quite glad about that.
Even when I think I know what I want and what I think would be best,
I sure wouldn't want to think I could call the shots!
That's a scary thought!
Oh, I understand that it's about relationship and how You want us to ask and all,
but I'm really seeing that it's much more than that."

God whispers, *"Oh Yes, Dear One, it is so much more.*
Always remember your purpose here on earth.
You have been created in My image and
called to manifest My presence and light in the world,
called to bring My Kingdom to earth as it is in heaven.
Prayer is how this comes about. And in truth, you are a prayer."

"I have freely given you good and perfect gifts,
everything you need for life and godliness." 2 Peter 1:3

Yes, I do see this...God has poured out lavish Love upon us,
filling us with the Spirit, and giving grace upon grace...
And yet our lives often lack love, lack power, lack grace.
What hinders us from receiving all that God has so freely given?
Certainly, the problem is not with God.
Something blocks the way for us to receive.
This is where prayer comes in...
Prayer is about making an opening for God's presence to flow into our world.
Prayer is about removing the hindrances to receiving.
Prayer is about opening the heart to see and know anew.

My contribution is faith...accepting that God desires to be intimately involved in my life.
But it's not my faith that affects change.
Faith helps to make the opening which becomes a channel or conduit for
God's power or grace or healing or truth or love to flow into the world.
God brings about the change...but I help "prepare the way"...
like John the Baptist prepared the way for Jesus the Christ.

"Prepare the way for God...the Kingdom of God is near." Mark 1:3,15
"...while he prayed, heaven opened." Luke 3:21

OUT OF YOUR HEART WILL FLOW RIVERS OF LIVING WATER

"Oh God, I feel pulled in different directions. There are needful things, good things, useful things.
There are demands from others. There are desires of my own.
They all pull at me creating tension.   I can't do it all.
Which things do I attend to? Which do I leave off?"

God whispers, *"Do you see that there are 'pulls' from within and 'pulls' from without?*
Look at all the possibilities.
Which ones reside or resonate from within your holy space...
that holy place of intimate communion with Me?
These are the ones that you accept and attend to.
The others need to be carefully considered but only accepted when clearly directed by My Spirit.
What resonates from within your holy space?"

Then I remembered Ezekiel's vision of the water flowing from the temple...
water that brought life and healing to all it touched.

"This water flows toward the east and goes down into the valley,
and enters the sea. When it reaches the sea, its waters are healed.
All living creatures along this river will live and thrive.
There will be an abundance of fish,
because of the healing water...
All kinds of trees will grow on the banks of the river, always producing fruit,
because the water flows from the sanctuary.
Their fruit will be for food, and their leaves for medicine."
Ezekiel 47:8-12

"It is the same for you...the water that brings life and healing must flow from the sanctuary...
that intimate place of communion with Me.
You are the temple of the Holy Spirit and out of your heart will flow life-giving water."

"Out of your heart will flow rivers of living water."
John 7:38

The challenge is shutting out the noise and commotion...both internal and external.
In the quietness and solitude,
I find my center and hear the whispers of my soul and the Spirit.

In that holy space, it comes to me...a knowing.

MY HEART LEAPS

"And I will give you a white stone,
and written on the stone will be your new name,
that only you will know."
Revelation 2:17

My heart leaps, "God, what's my name?"

I thought about names. God has many names in scripture...
Names that often express the heart and character of God:
Jehovah Jireh (God My Provider), Jehovah Rapha (God My Healer),
Lahai Roi (The God Who Lives and Sees)

Later, as I prayed for a friend, I was given a glimpse of God's heart toward her.
God whispered, *"She is my great delight"*.
"Is that my friend's name? 'My Great Delight'?"

I knew that God did take great delight in my friend,
but I also realized that she took great delight in God...God was her great delight.
She was also a great delight to me. Yes, certainly, that was one of her names.

Soon afterwards, God gave me a glimpse into his heart for me.

I entered the unit at the jail with the ministry team and right away I saw her...
the young woman about whom I had been so concerned.
Her life had been in danger when she had been released a few weeks before.
When I saw her, my heart leapt!
I raced to her and gave her a hug and said, "I am so glad to see you!"

In that moment, God whispered to my heart: *"My Heart Leaps when I see you."*
And I could see also that it was indeed my heart toward God...
My Heart Leaps in response to God.

(What's your name? Do you share a name with some of my other friends? "Great Desire",
"Cherished in the Secret Place", "My Heart Pursues", "Close to My Heart"?)

I am often reminded of the name I was given: "My Heart Leaps".
It is my response to God's presence in my life...
and God's response to me.

ENTER THE DEPTHS

"The deep calls to me in the roaring waters;
Your waves sweep over me and possess me."
Psalm 42:7

What is it about the ocean that is so intriguing…so enticing?

I suppose it is the mystery of it…so vast…so deep…so powerful.
Suddenly, I am very aware of my vulnerability,
my humanness, my mortality.
Oh, how very finite and small I am.
And yet there is great comfort and peace.
Is it to know that I am not the center of the universe?
Is it to know I am powerless?
Is it to know there is something…
Someone…
greater, mightier, more infinite…who calls to me?

"God, it is so amazing…so incredible…
and yet frightening.
As I become more intimately aware of my vulnerability,
I am drawn to You in a greater way.
It really doesn't make sense.
Why would I be drawn to what is so unknown…
so powerful…so consuming?"

God whispers, *"Oh, dear one, I am calling to the very depth of your soul.*
For deep in your soul is the knowledge that
You are a part of Me.
I gave you life and breath …
Your place is with Me…in Me."

As I touch the deep reality of my own mortal soul,
I am drawn to the deep reality of the eternal, infinite, mighty God
Who draws me into the ebb and flow of Divine mystery.

"God is mightier than the roaring waters,
powerful and relentless like the waves of the sea."
Psalm 93:4

I WILL NOT LEAVE YOU COMFORTLESS

"You know, God, this passage has been different.
　　　　The grief and anger are there...
　　　　　　　　it's real but somehow quieter, gentler.
It doesn't consume me like it would have done in the past.
I'm not in crisis...
　　　　I'm feeling it but it doesn't possess me or identify me...it just is."

And I bring it to God, like a little child brings an injured bird to her mother saying,
　　　　"Oh, look, her wing is broken, how do we help her get well?"
And so they keep her warm and safe and care for her
　　　　　　　　until the wing heals and she is ready to fly again.

God whispers, *"Yes, dear one, this is how you trust Me in the midst of your pain.*
　　　　You bring it to Me in just this way only it's all within.
　　　　　　　　You bring it to My indwelling Spirit...
　　　　　　　　　　　　that internal Presence within you...
　　　　　　　My Holy Spirit...
　　　　　　　　　　　　Who comforts, helps, and nurtures you along your way.
And do not think that there is anything too small to bring...
　　　　I care about every detail of your life and desire to be with you in it all."

"I will pray and ask God to give you another Comforter,
　　　　who will be with you always.
　　　God dwells with you, and will be in you.
　　I will not leave you comfortless: I will come to you."
John 14:16-18

"Nothing happens that I don't know about it...
even something like a tiny sparrow falling to the ground.
Or the number of hairs on your head.
So don't be afraid;
you are more valuable to Me than a whole flock of sparrows."
Matthew 10:29-31

OH, THE JOY I HAVE IN YOU!

K. Doerge

"I will rejoice over you. You will rest in My love;
I will sing and be joyful about you."
Zephaniah 3:17

"God, it's really hard to imagine what that's like:
You rejoicing and singing over me.
And what's to be joyful about?"

God whispers, "*You know your little buddy, Cole, in the church nursery?*
Tell me about him."

"Oh, God, he is such a winsome little guy.
I smile to think of him...his bright eyes and sweet smile.
Even when he's being a little rascal, he's such a delight!
I love to watch him 'flex his muscles'.
His enthusiasm and sense of adventure
bring life to all those around him.
It's amazing to see him 'becoming'...
like watching a flower open."

"Now do you understand the joy I have in you?
I smile to think of you...your bright eyes and sweet smile.
Even when you're 'being a rascal',
I take delight in you,
for I know that even in your testing and wandering,
you are learning and growing
and will return to Me just as the prodigal did.
I love to watch you 'flex your muscles'
trying new things...reaching further and higher.
And you too are 'becoming'.
Yes, like a flower opening. "

"Oh, the joy I have in you!"

"Don't you know you are my dear child, the child in whom I delight?
I am always thinking of you.
My heart yearns for you and is filled with compassion for you."
Jeremiah 31:20

WHO TOUCHED ME?

K. Doerge

I've heard the story many times..the woman with the "issue of blood"
and how she knew that if she just touched the hem of Jesus' garment,
she would be healed.
The image of her reaching out to touch Jesus is intimate and powerful.

But as I looked more closely,
I realized that I had overlooked perhaps the most important part of the story.
This story is not so much about this woman and her faith and healing...
it is about Jesus and His heart and desire for us.
After the woman touches the hem of Jesus' garment and is healed,
Jesus asks, "Who touched me?" Oh, I think He knew who touched Him but
He wanted her to know that He knew...that He saw her...
and that he knew her deepest need.
Jesus turns to look for her,

"And when the woman realized that she could not hide, she came to Him..." Luke 8:47

Jesus doesn't let her stay hidden...He pursues her...He looks for her.
She tries to take her healing and leave...but He has so much more for her.
He wants her to know that He sees her...that He knows her...
and that the healing is freely hers.
He calls her daughter...He affirms her...He gives her a blessing.
Oh, He had so much more for her.

But then I realize that I often approach God in a similar way...
I'm going for a "hit and run" experience
rather than opening myself to having an intimate encounter with God.
In a way, I touch the hem of God's garment
when I receive something from scripture, or worship, or people of faith, or beauty...
But God wants so much more for me.

"I think I'm catching on God.
You want me to know that You know...that You see me...that You know what I need.
You want to call me daughter and encourage me...
You want to bless me. Pretty amazing!"

God whispers, *"You know, Dear One, you are never hidden from my sight. I see you.*
I know your deepest need. I am always with you.
I don't mind playing "hide and seek" with you, as long as you let yourself be found.
But some times you run off before we can spend time together.
So don't hurry away next time...I have so much for you."

My Gifts Are For Keeps

My heart cries, "God, it's hard to let go!
Oh, I do pretty well with letting go of damaging, harmful things...
It can be a pain process to realize that I've become attached to something that's not good...
But You give me grace and strength to release my grasp and I'm glad to let go."

"But, what's hard is letting go of the good things...the lovely things...
things that were a gift from You.
Do You really want me to do that?"

"Hey, wait a minute...I don't even know if that's scriptural!
If You gave it to me, it's mine and I don't have to give it back!"

In my heart, I knew it was time to let go...
I knew God was prompting me to give up this thing that was so dear
like opening my hand to release a bird to freedom.
But oh, how I wanted to hold on to what was mine...to this precious gift.

God whispers, *"Read the story of Hannah."*

Dear, dear Hannah, a woman in anguish and sorrow but God met her there.
God gave her the desire of her heart...
a son whom she released back to God at the proper time.
For you see, Hannah's heart was focused on the "Gift Giver", not the gift.
The Gift Giver had taken away her reproach, her sorrow, her despair.
She had no confusion about this.

"I prayed for this child,
and God gave me what I asked for.
So now I give him back to God for the rest of his life."
1 Samuel 1:27

Hannah gave the child to God...but the gift was hers to keep.
The real gift was that the Lord had removed her reproach...
this gift was hers always.

God whispers, *"See, you will never lose the real gift.*
What I worked in your life, will always be yours.
But by letting go of the 'vessel',
your hands are ready to receive new gifts which I delight to give."

Don't Lose Sight of Your Destination

"God, You've been so faithful to provide for me.
But, God, how I want to hold on!
I know I must receive what you have for me today with no demand for tomorrow.
I cannot own or possess it. I must trust You.
Is this just an exercise in faith?"

God whispers, *"No, dear child, this is not just an exercise in faith though your faith will grow.*
Do you remember what I told you about letting go of the 'vessel'
so that your hands are ready to receive new gifts which I delight to give?
You are on a journey. There are twists and turns,
dangers and hazards,
distractions and enticements.
You don't know what is ahead...but I do.
I provide what you need for each step of your journey.
You must let go of yesterday's provision
in order to receive what you need for today and for tomorrow.
Don't lose sight of your destination."

The words of Psalm 121 came to mind.

Lift up your eyes to the hills—where does your help come from?
Your help comes from Me, creator of heaven and earth.
I will make sure that you don't lose your footing: I am the One who takes care of you.
I am always on the job, I neither slumber nor sleep.
I am your keeper; your shelter at your right hand.
Day and night, I am protecting you,
I preserve you from all evil; I preserve your soul.
I watch over your going out and your coming in, now and always.

Oh, yes, a good reminder: God is the One who guides me, keeps me, and covers me
as I journey. Psalm 121 is one of the Songs of Ascents that the children of Israel
sang as they journeyed up to Jerusalem to worship. They would lift their eyes to the hills
for that was their destination: Jerusalem, the city of God, set on a hill.
They did not lose sight of their destination. Likewise, we also journey
in the upward call of God...with God guiding us, keeping us, and covering us.

"I press on and pursue with passion, the upward call to the fullness of God in Christ."
Philippians 3:14

I Know, I See

This story of Hagar out in the desert is very moving.

> Hagar...seemingly a "nobody" in the scheme of things...
>> worse than a "nobody"...forsaken, rejected, discounted..
> But not by God.

God comes to her and speaks to her in her aloneness and despair.

> God doesn't fix her situation...
> but Hagar is deeply and profoundly impacted by God's presence.

And Hagar gives God a name:

> "Lahai Roi", "The God Who Lives and Sees Me" (Genesis 16:13)

What a powerful, life-changing encounter...

> experiencing the reality of God seeing me.

And amazingly, as I experience God seeing me, I see myself in a greater way.

It's seems foolish to think that God doesn't see me...

> for some reason I think I can be unseen or hidden.

As I embrace this very intimate truth...that God knows and sees,

> I realize that not only can I not hide from God,
>> I cannot hide from myself or God's calling on my life.

"God I do know that You see me.

> I know that You saw me before I was ever born
>> and know more about me than I know about myself.

Though it would help if You'd make Yourself a little more obvious at times."

God whispers, *"I'll keep that in mind!*

> *And here's something for you to keep in mind:*
>> *Listen for Me, watch for Me. I am always with you,*
>> *intimately aware and present.*
> *As you encounter Me (The-God-Who-Lives-and-Sees),*
>> *you'll find yourself and see more clearly your purpose and calling.*
>> *Be assured, I know, I see."*

> "Can I go anywhere and Your Spirit not be there?
> Or could I ever be out of Your sight?
> You saw me before I was born, as I took form in my mother's womb.
> You knew everything about me and my life before I took my first breath."
> Psalm 139:7,15-16

COME AWAY BY YOURSELF

"And Jesus said to them,
'Come away by yourselves to a secluded place and rest a while.'"
Mark 6:31

"God, I know you are calling me to that solitary place.
I'm not really afraid but it's uncomfortable... unfamiliar and hidden.
And others don't understand."

I remember the imagery of the forest and my painting that sat and waited for so long.

Now I see that it is time to enter into this place of hiddeness.
It is a place of safety and refuge
but also one of transformation and birth.
It is a secret place
where much growth and change takes place... unseen.

The "beasts of the field" meet and feast in the open meadow.
But then they are drawn into the forest, not just for safety and protection,
but to rest,
to heal,
to give birth.
All of this takes place in the darkness, covered and sheltered...
in the hidden secret place.
Life-giving light sprinkles in softly, gently...
as transformation takes place under God's protective canopy.

God whispers, *"Come away, My Beloved...*
to this secret place I have prepared for you.
Here you will find rest and healing...
vision and hope."

"Therefore, I will allure you,
and bring you into the wilderness, and speak comfort to you.
I will return your vineyards to you there,
and the Valley of Trouble will become a door of hope;
You will sing there, as in the days of your youth,
as in the day when you came up from captivity."
Hosea 2:14,15

I Will Lead You Home

K. Doerge

"God, how do we forget our native language? How do we forget that we come from
a distant place and that our true home is with You?
That we existed in Your heart long before we existed in this world.
How is it that we have given up our birthright and
have forgotten that we were created by You, for You, in You in eternity, for eternity?"

Perhaps we occasionally hear that distant call...a piece of music, the words of a song or poem,
shimmering with eternity...or we see it...in the beauty of nature...
in the innocence and sweetness of a newborn baby...

But so often we let it pass without entering through the opening...
a door leading us back home...back to God's heart.
But then there is a painful reality for those who do respond, who do venture in
to reclaim their birthright.
For suddenly, we realize that we don't belong to this world...
that we came from and journey toward another place.
Our "native language" is the language of the heart sung into us before we were born.

So we seek out others who speak our "native language" who travel with us in our journey home.
We search for those who haven't completely forgotten...
who can help us remember the parts we've forgotten
and we in turn help them remember the parts they've forgotten.
So that together we may reclaim our birthright and fulfill the purpose for which we were created.

It's kind of lonely though...so many have forgotten...and sometimes we find others
who seem to remember but sadly the language has become confused and garbled.

And we feel a barrenness as we long for home.

God whispers, *"Yes, dear one, it can be barren and lonely at times...
and full of longing as you look for a better place...your spiritual homeland.
Remember My promises... I will lead you home."*

"They lived by faith
and even though they didn't receive the fulfillment of God's promises in this life,
they saw them in the future. They admitted that they didn't belong here...
they were seeking an eternal home. They yearned for their true home with God.
God is pleased to be their God and has prepared a city for them."
Hebrews 11:13-16

Devotional Helps

To use this book as a devotional or with a group, duplicate the journaling sheet on the facing page and use it to guide you through each graphic psalm.

There are 40 graphic psalms included in this collection which lend themselves well to a lenten devotional or other 40-day intentional focus.

Journaling Sheet

Read the graphic psalm through slowly. Write down the words or passages that touch you, confuse, attract or disturb you.

_____

_____

_____

Can you recall a similar time in your own life? What were the circumstances?

_____

_____

List the names of people who come to mind as you read and reflect on the graphic psalm.

_____

_____

Read the psalm through again, putting yourself in the psalmist's place. Let the psalm come alive for you.
What emotions does it trigger? What desires or longings arise?

_____

_____

Write out the title of the graphic psalm: _____
Listen for God to speak these words to you personally.

Read the Scripture passages included in the graphic psalm. (Look them up in your favorite translation.)
Meditate on the image for several minutes, allowing it to permeate your spirit.

Openly and honestly express your heart to God. Share your joys and concerns. Whisper to God's heart, the names of those who came to mind reading this psalm. Sit in silence, resting quietly in God's presence. Journal your experience and reflections.

_____

_____

_____

_____

_____

_____

About The Author

Katherine Doerge is an artist, writer, and spiritual director
in Arlington, Texas.
She received her spiritual direction training through the
Anglican School of Theology in Dallas, Texas and the
Pecos Benedictine Monastery's School for Spiritual Direction
in Pecos, New Mexico.

You can contact her through her website: www.myheartleaps.com

Made in the USA
Columbia, SC
19 May 2017